All About the
TURTLE

A Sterling Color Nature Book

William White, Jr., Ph.D.

 Sterling Publishing Co., Inc.   New York

Library of Congress Cataloging-in-Publication Data

White, William, 1954–
   All about the turtle / William White, Jr.
      p.   cm. — (A Sterling color nature book)
   "Portions of this work are adapted from A turtle is born"—T.p.
verso.
   Includes index.
   Summary: Discusses turtles in ancient times and their physical
characteristics, habits, and life cycle today.
   ISBN 0-8069-8276-4
   1. Turtles—Juvenile literature. [1. Turtles.] I. Title
II. Series.
QL666.C5W48   1992
597.92—dc20   91–41301
                                      CIP
                                      AC

10 9 8 7 6 5 4 3 2 1

Published by Sterling Publishing Company, Inc.
387 Park Avenue South, New York, N.Y. 10016
© 1992 by William White, Jr.
Portions of this work are adapted from
A Turtle Is Born by William White, Jr, © 1973
by Sterling Publishing Company
Distributed in Canada by Sterling Publishing
% Canadian Manda Group, P.O. Box 920, Station U
Toronto, Ontario, Canada M8Z 5P9
Distributed in Great Britain and Europe by Cassell PLC
Villiers House, 41/47 Strand, London WC2N 5JE, England
Distributed in Australia by Capricorn Link Ltd.
P.O. Box 665, Lane Cove, NSW 2066
Printed and bound in Hong Kong

Sterling 0-8069-8276-4

Contents

1. *A small reedy pond by a farm field. Here turtles, frogs, and sunfish occupy the top of the food chain.*

1. What Is a Turtle?

A turtle is easy enough to describe. It is a four-legged reptile covered top and bottom by a bony shell. It is a *vertebrate* with its backbone partly fused to the shell. All four of its limbs are connected inside its ribs unlike any other vertebrate.

Turtles are "cold-blooded," which means that their bodies produce very little heat, so they take on the temperature of their environment. Cold-blooded animals are called *poikilotherms* by scientists.

All turtles are wider than they are high and most can withdraw their heads, tails, and four limbs into their shells to some extent. All turtles hatch from leathery eggs and must lay their eggs on dry land. When we once see a turtle we can see it is different and distinct from any other kind of animal.

Turtles are related in many ways to other familiar reptiles and amphibians, such as frogs, lizards and even snakes, although snakes have no legs.

2. *The top shell or carapace of a young Map Turtle of the central United States.*

3. *The bottom shell or plastron of a young Map Turtle.*

6   *All About the Turtle*

2. How Did Turtles Get Their Name?

Some confusion exists about the use of the three common English language names for turtle, which are: *turtle, tortoise,* and *terrapin.*

When British explorers began to sail to distant lands in the 1600's and 1700's, they caught sight of various kinds of turtles for the first time, as there were none in the British Isles. The sailors were familiar with the French word for turtle, *tortue.* But the English language had a similar sounding name for another animal, actually, a bird, the *turtle dove.* So *turtle* became the common name for the new reptile.

A French word was also used for the same reptile, *tortoise.* A variation of this same word in its Spanish form became the name of the "turtle islands" in the West Indies, the *Tortugas.* The first English settlers in Virginia called the small aquatic turtles of the area *terrapin,* which seems to have been another form of the French word. In common usage, *turtle* became the general name, while *tortoise* is used for the dry-land species, and *terrapin* is applied to the edible aquatic varieties.

However, none of these names has any specific scientific meaning. Scientists give each turtle species the usual naturalist's set of two names derived from Greek and Latin. For example, the common North American Painted Turtle, which is found throughout the whole continent, has the scientific name *Chrysemys picta.*

The upper shell of turtles is called a *carapace* (ILLUSTRATION 2). This usually covers the entire top of the turtle and gives it an added overhang to protect the neck, tail, and limbs.

The lower shell of turtles is called a *plastron,* and is much smaller and has no projections. (ILLUSTRATION 3.)

The carapace is made up of bony plates which are actually flattened ribs that are fused to the vertebrae. Over these plates of bone, there are tough horny plates, called *lamina*, or usually known as *scutes*. Thus, the carapace of the turtle is extremely durable and resists all kinds of wear and tear.

The plastron is made up of similar layers of bony plates and scutes, but is much smaller in area. (ILLUSTRATION 3.) There are side bars of bone which connect the carapace to the plastron on the sides of the turtle. These are usually called *bridges*.

The turtle's ribs are fused to the carapace. Male turtles usually have a slightly depressed or concave plastron, while female turtles have a slightly extended, curved, or convex plastron.

The carapace of male turtles is often more extended than that of females of the same species. The plastron of females is often larger than that of males of the same species. The colors of male turtles are also usually brighter. The eye color of the sexes also differs in many species. The eyes of females are usually green to brown, while those of males may be bright yellow or even red. The eyes of male turtles are said to turn brighter during the mating season, but this has not been proved. Males do become much more active during the mating and egg-producing season.

The head of the turtle is very solid, with few openings in the sides of the skull. These indentations are what scientists call *temporal openings*. The skulls of turtles have an almost rounded and compact shape. (ILLUSTRATION 5).

Only three features are visible, the mouth, the large eyes and the two nostrils. There are no external ears. (ILLUSTRATION 6).

The skull is as simple and compact inside as it is outside. It is completely roofed over for strength and is connected to the carapace by a long "S"-shaped neck. (ILLUSTRATION 7 and 8.)

Turtles have no teeth, but have beaks similar to birds. These have saw-toothed edges called *serrations* and can be very sharp.

If turtles withdraw their heads into their shells by pulling straight back and forming a vertical "S" they are classed as *Cryptodira*. If they withdraw their heads into their shells by forming the "S" loop sideways, that is, horizontally, they are classed as *Pleurodira*. These are the two major divisions of turtles.

While turtles may seem terribly clumsy inside their thick

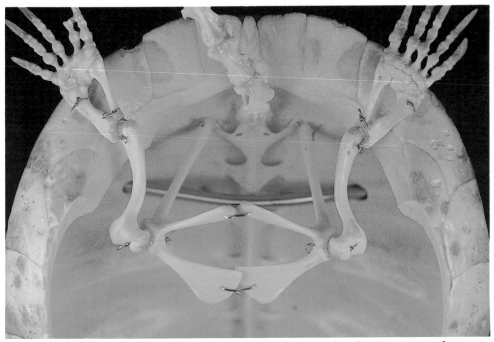

4. *The inside of the fore end of the carapace with the plastron removed. The fused ribs and the shoulder bones and limbs inside the ribs are clearly seen.*

5. *The round, roofed-over head of a large Galapagos Tortoise.*

6. *The alert eyes and nostrils of a small pond turtle watching the photographer and looking for a place to escape.*

boxes of bone, the head and long neck give them the ease of movement and ability to do most things other animals would do with their paws. The skull and neck work together to accomplish this trick. (ILLUSTRATION 8.)

In fact, turtles' necks are so long and their heads so strong, that all but the heaviest turtles can flip themselves over right side up from being on their backs. They push down with their heads on the ground, while they right their bodies by twisting their necks.

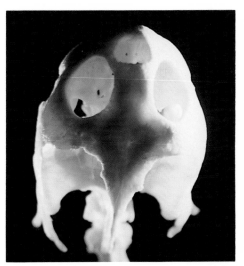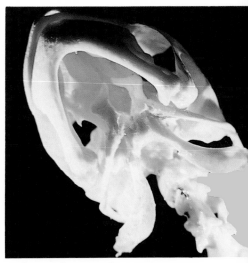

7. A large freshwater turtle skull from above, showing the prominent eye sockets and opening of the nostrils. But note how there are no ear openings.

8. The underside of the skull in ILLUSTRATION 7, showing the long neck connected in the middle of the skull. The upper and lower halves of the beak are shown and the powerful jawbone.

9. The Eastern Painted Turtle is here sunning itself with its legs stretched out over a small pond. This is one of most common turtles of North America.

10. A very small pond turtle is king of all it surveys in this tiny world of mud and swamp plants.

3. Where Do Turtles Live?

Turtles live throughout the temperate regions of the world, on many continents and islands. About 300 species of turtles exist in the world, and about 45 species are found in the United States and Canada, while none are found in the British Isles. Most of the species which live in North America and Europe are primarily river varieties. A common sight almost anywhere on a hot summer day in North America is a group of Painted Turtles perched on a rock or log to sun themselves. Turtle varieties thrive throughout almost all of the river systems of the United States.

Pond turtles are usually the largest vertebrates in their aquatic environment, and they enjoy a vast variety of foods with virtually no enemies other than dogs, cats, and humans. The quiet ponds

11. *The surface of this Southern swamp is choked with duckweed but it is full of tadpoles and insect larvae. Amid the duckweed is a large Spider Turtle ready to feed on the abundance of plants and animals.*

found at the edges of farm fields and even along suburban housing are the "nursery" where hundreds of thousands of aquatic turtles grow and mature (ILLUSTRATION 10.)

But in the minds of most people, it is the swamp where reptiles and amphibians of all kinds abound. Since more and more wetlands are being drained for building development and farming, this very valuable habitat is fast disappearing. Shallow weed-choked areas of slow-moving, or standing water, are a frequent haunt for turtles of all kinds. (ILLUSTRATION 11.) In such environments, you will have to keep a sharp eye to see the turtles at all, as they take advantage of the thick vegetation to hide in wait for prey and stay hidden from their few enemies.

Turtles are also very well adapted to other environments. One of the most common habitats in North America and Europe is the woodland. As in the swamp, the heavy undergrowth on the forest floor and the many rocks and roots provide hiding places and an

12. *The Box Turtle or Tortoise, a woodland dweller at three stages in its life cycle. These attractive little turtles live all of their lives in the woods among the leaf fall and underbrush.*

abundance of food. This environment is particularly important for the small tortoises, such as the common Box Turtle. (ILLUSTRA-TION 12.) This species is unique in having a hinge across the middle of its plastron which allows it to withdraw all its limbs and close up tight to withstand any curious dog or child. Its early stages are secretive—turtles live out their first year or so in the matted leaf fall at the base of the trees.

Another habitat to which turtles have adapted with marked success is the desert. Throughout the North American, Asian, and African deserts there are varieties of tortoises. These are dependent on the scant vegetation and large numbers of insects for survival. Generally, the dry land species have higher and rounder carapaces and can move themselves higher above the ground in their wanderings. (ILLUSTRATION 13.) An African land tortoise is typical of the species which inhabit the desert and dry grasslands called savannas. Some of the desert varieties can even pass into brief hibernation-like states, called *estivation*, when the weather conditions become too hot and dry. (ILLUSTRATION 14.)

13. *The desert seems the most inhospitable place for turtles, but actually many species thrive here.*

14. *A typical desert tortoise with its heavy legs and high-domed carapace.*

15. *This young Map Turtle has withdrawn into its shell. It can also with-draw its tail in a side-wrapping motion.*

15a. *The Diamond-Backed Terrapin forages both salt and freshwater shores, bays and swamps for its wide variety of food. It prefers mollusks of all types, small crabs, clams, and mussels, but will eat fish and insects. Since its food supply is so rich and varied, it is a very successful and plentiful species.*

The largest turtles that have ever lived, and the largest now living, are those that inhabit the sea. Turtles have been on earth for at least 200 million years, from the period before the dinosaurs. Some sea turtle fossils measure 12 feet (3.6m) in length and must have weighed many tons as they swam with enormous paddle-like limbs through the ancient seas. The sea turtles are the most famous as they return every year to a few areas of tropical beaches in great numbers to lay their eggs in the sand. On occasion, they will veer off course and nest many hundreds of miles away from their destination.

There are a few small sea turtles, but most marine species are larger than any land species. The largest living turtle is the Leatherback which attains a shell length of 6 feet (2m), a width across the flippers of 12 feet (3.5m) and a weight of 1½ tons. Very little is known about its habits, although its young, only a few inches long, have been found in vast masses of seaweed floating in the Gulf of Mexico and off the northern coast of Brazil. Here they hide in the dense growth of kelp, and feed on the plants and animals which thrive among the mats. More typical sea turtles such as the Green Turtle grow to less than 3 feet in length.

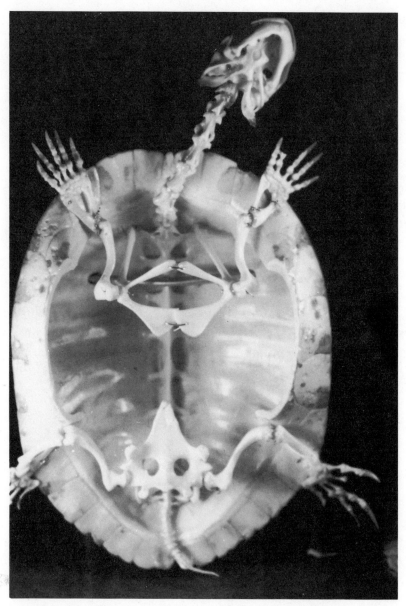

16. A full view of the turtle skeleton with the plastron removed to show the bones of the shoulder and pelvic regions.

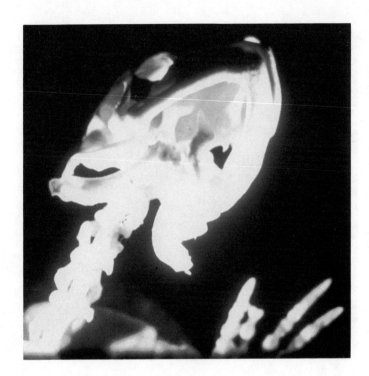

17. The skull and extensive neck bones of a Cryptodira-type turtle which enable it to withdraw its head straight into its shell.

4. How Do Turtles Live?

Turtles can survive in all different kinds of environments—from tiny shallow ponds to parched deserts and great oceans—by having special adaptations. As we saw, the turtle's first and most obvious characteristic is its box-like protective body form, seen best in the skeleton. (ILLUSTRATION 16.) This makes it very safe, but rigid, so the turtle has a number of marvelous adaptations to provide it with movements and abilities. The quick withdrawal of the vital organs in its head for protection is its chief concern. (ILLUSTRATIONS 15 and 17.)

Even in those varieties which cannot completely close the carapace or plastrom over their head, the vital organs can be drawn in far enough so they cannot be bitten or clawed by potential predators. But more often than not, it is the mating

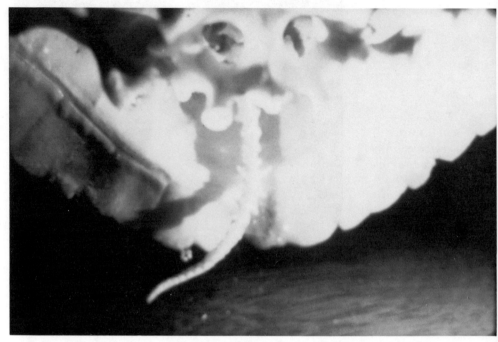

18. *The tail vertebrae and pelvic girdle bones are attached to the inside of the carapace, making it difficult for a turtle to draw its tail straight back.*

battles between individuals of the same species which cause the most injury.

The head and neck are particulary well fitted for the protective movement. (ILLUSTRATION 17.) But equally necessary is the withdrawal of the tail and its reproductive organs. (ILLUSTRATION 18.) The rear portion of the skeleton and the overhang of the carapace provide for this.

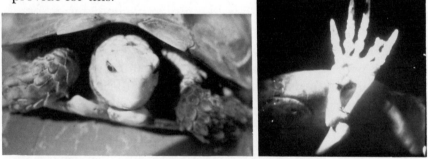

19. *The forefeet of turtles that forage on land have birdlike claws, as seen here in the African tortoise, and in (20) the skeleton of a forefoot.*

Not only can American Box Turtles and some aquatic species close up their plastron, but some African species can also close up the back of their carapace to completely cover their tails. The head and tail are withdrawn simultaneously in most species. Unlike the head, the tail cannot be drawn straight back even in the Cryptodira. (ILLUSTRATION 18.) But as turtles grow older and often get heavier, they seem less able to withdraw their heads and appendages into their shells.

The placement of a turtle's forelegs forces it into a side-to-side walking style—this is accompanied by moving the head from side to side to test the air, to both smell and taste it.

The most perfect adaptations of the turtle are usually over-looked. The shape of the clawed front and back limbs is partic-ularly important. Turtles which forage on land usually have bird-like claws and scale limbs with specialized bones to aid in move-ment. (ILLUSTRATIONS 19 AND 20.) The number of digits (fingers or toes) may vary from one species to another, the smallest number being two, the greatest five. (ILLUSTRATIONS 21 AND 23.)

The freshwater and ocean species have flippers which resem-ble those of seals and sea lions. They are connected and very much longer than the limbs of the land-dwelling species. As a result, many large sea turtles have great difficulty pulling them-selves up on the beaches where they dig nests and lay their eggs. While they are magnificent swimmers and perfectly adapted for life in water, sea turtles are completely out of their environment on land.

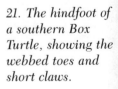

21. The hindfoot of a southern Box Turtle, showing the webbed toes and short claws.

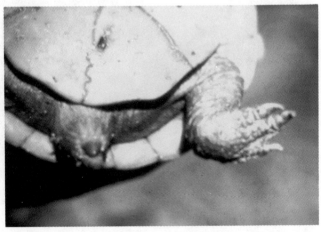

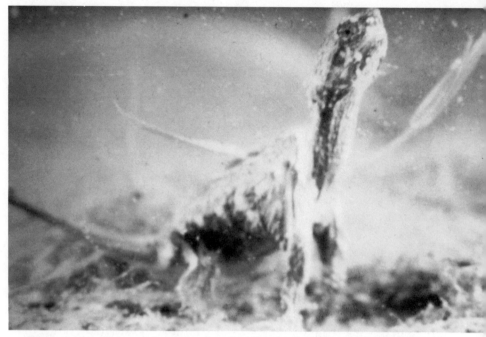

22. *A young Alligator Snapping Turtle only 3 inches long rises from the pond bottom on its fully extended legs. It thrusts its head with its long neck extended the full length of its body, then it pushes its nostrils just above the water surface and inhales, exhales, and inhales, some fresh air.*

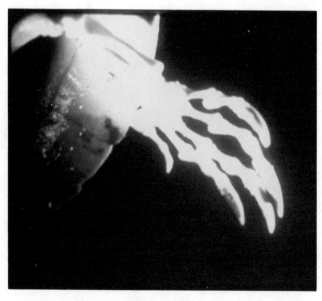

23. *The well-developed skeleton of a pond turtle's hindfoot, showing the five toes and long claws.*

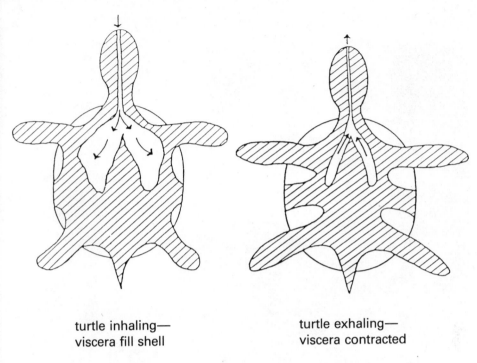

turtle inhaling—
viscera fill shell

turtle exhaling—
viscera contracted

24. Respiratory system of the turtle.

5. What Do Turtles Have in Common?

All turtles have in common the way in which they take in and expel oxygen, the way in which they breathe. Unlike mammals and birds, turtles cannot pump air in and out of their lungs by moving their ribs. Inside their box-like skeletons, they must move their internal organs by contracting and expanding their muscles. But where mammals, including humans, tense their muscles to expand their lungs and relax their muscles to contract their lungs, turtles do just the opposite. They tense their muscles to exhale and relax their muscles to inhale. (ILLUSTRATION 24.)

25. *Cold-blooded, this pond turtle is half in sun and half in shade as it seeks to cool itself off. The turtle's temperature changes as the temperature of the air and water in its immediate environment changes throughout the day.*

Aside from this, there are many other special adaptations among turtles for obtaining and conserving oxygen. Turtles use very much less oxygen for their body weight than almost any other vertebrates. Aquatic species can obtain oxygen from water through areas in their throats—even their *cloacae* or rectums! This allows them to stay submerged in a pond, river, or ocean, for hours, days, and even weeks at a time without coming up for a breath.

Those species which live in shallow swamps, where very little oxygen is dissolved in the water, often have extra long necks. This enables them to make a quick poke of their head to the surface to catch an occasional gulp of fresh air. (ILLUSTRATION 22.)

Turtles have other internal adaptations also. While their hearts are smaller and less developed than those of mammals, and they are able to pump less, they can survive on less oxygen. The entire chemical system of turtles, including their circulation, runs at a much slower rate than that of many other animals. This may be one of the reasons why they are the most long-lived of all animals.

Since turtles are poikilotherms, that is *cold-blooded*, they take on the temperature of the environment wherever they are. This is one reason why their range is limited to temperate climates, and the majority live in the tropics. If you watch any turtle throughout the day you will find it gets more active as the sun heats the air or water around it, and its temperature rises. (ILLUS-TRATION 25.)

Turtles need sunlight to survive, as they can and must produce vitamin A which requires sunshine. In the desert, however, as the day grows hotter they must seek shade. So many desert varieties such as the Gopher Tortoise are good tunnel diggers— they can hide under the warm sand and out of the bright rays of the sun. A typical pond turtle will stay in or near water at all times, not only to keep moist but also to maintain its tempera-ture, as water heats and cools slower than air. Desert tortoises have higher shells and can raise themselves on their heavy legs higher off the ground than aquatic varieties. This allows them to cool their bodies better. Often, they will simply stand motionless on all fours and let air circulate under and around them.

27. *A small pond turtle is moving through the underbrush foraging for food. It will eat almost anything: worms, beetles, fungi, plant shoots, and berries.*

28. *One of the most voracious feeders among all turtles, the common American Snapping Turtle continually forages the swamps and ponds where it makes its home. It eats anything it can catch, from fish and frogs to ducks and squirrels. It will also eat mollusks and insects and even water plants when necessary.*

6. What Do Turtles Eat?

Turtles eat almost anything. While different species differ widely in what they prefer, some kinds of turtles eat virtually any kind of foodstuffs from fallen leaves to dead animals. Since their typical environment in North America is freshwater, most American turtles eat anything that grows in rivers and ponds. When left to themselves, turtles stay on a continual hunt for food. Their two chief means of locating it are their eyes and smell, the two most prominent sense organs in the head. While temperature and moisture conditions are favorable in their environment, they forage slowly for food. (ILLUSTRATION 27.) The overwhelming majority of turtle species feed on animal material while they are small, and on plants when they are adult. This is especially true of the giant tortoises and sea turtles.

Those turtles which live in brackish water, a mixture of salt and freshwater along bays and estuaries, have the choice of vast quantities of small shellfish, fish, and seaweed. (ILLUSTRATION 33.) Along the eastern coast of North America the Diamond-Backed Terrapin, so highly prized for human food since the days of the first English settlers, is the most common brackish water species.

But other turtles are strictly carnivorous. One of the best examples is the Snapping Turtle of the swamps of North America. (ILLUSTRATION 28.) It is a large species, found wherever there is sufficient water. It frequently lives under ice in the northern part of its range. Called "snapping" because of its vicious and aggressive temper, it can hardly withdraw its head completely, or even partially into its shell. It fights off most potential enemies, and bites anything which moves close to it.

The author once kept a 25-pound male in a large rain barrel in North Carolina, where these turtles would frequently travel through the garden after a heavy rainstorm. One evening, the

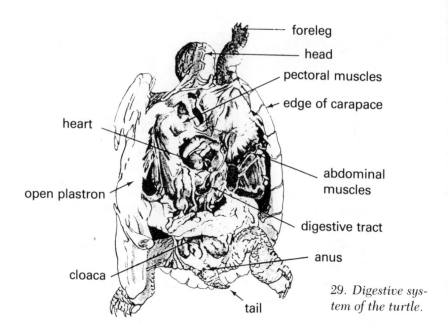

foreleg
head
pectoral muscles
edge of carapace
heart
abdominal muscles
open plastron
digestive tract
anus
cloaca
tail

29. Digestive system of the turtle.

turtle actually managed to pull a full-grown squirrel into its rain barrel, and had it half eaten in a few hours.

But the all-time example of aggression among turtles is the Alligator Snapping Turtle of the southern United States. It has a rougher shell than the more common variety of Snapper, and grows to be the largest of all freshwater turtles in the world. Individuals over 3 feet in length, weighing over 200 pounds, with heads fully 2 feet in width, are not uncommon. These turtles, very vicious and voracious, can easily bite off a dog's foot or a human finger or toe with ease. They eat almost all animal matter exclusively, and feast on frogs and fish.

The way they catch fish is a most interesting adaptation. A tiny bright pink appendage attached to their tongue resembles a worm when their mouth is popped open. They will lie underwater for hours with this appendage the only part of their body moving until some inquisitive fish swims close enough to investigate. Then they snap their jaws closed on their prey and soon gulp it down. The snap of the jaws of a large turtle of this species may be so hard that a distinctive crack, like a rat trap closing, can be heard far under the water surface. Even newly-hatched Alligator Snapping Turtles share the fierce snapping habits of the older specimens.

30. *This small young Alligator Snapping Turtle, only 2½ inches (6.5cm) long is already practicing its species' method of hunting its prey by opening its hooked beak and luring in small water animals with its lure-like tongue which resembles some kind of pink worm. This little turtle will grow on its almost pure carnivorous diet to over 100 pounds.*

31. *The strange and bizarre Matamata is unique in its flat, pitted shell and exceedingly broad neck. It feeds by sucking down all types of water animals into its enormous mouth and then swallowing them into its powerfully muscled stomach.*

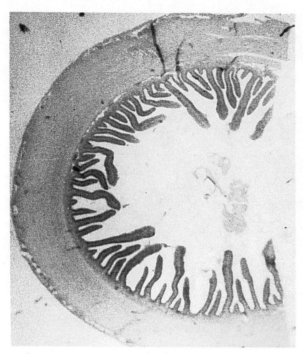

32. *A microscopic cross-section of a part of a turtle's intestine showing the bands of muscle which move the partly digested mass through its digestive tract, and the fine finger-like projections through which the liquid food is finally absorbed into the bloodstream.*

Turtles have still other unusual adaptations for feeding in their environments. Some feed extensively on snails, others on crabs and other crustacea. But the weird Matamata (ILLUSTRATION 31), a freshwater species of stagnant ponds and swamps of Brazil and Guyana, has a number of strange and bizarre features. It is about 18 inches (42cm) in length and very flat, with a greatly reduced plastron. Its carapace, however, is rough and knobby and actually is somewhat soft, so that it develops holes and uneven edges. These become covered with algae and totally disguise the turtle on the bottom of its habitat. The head is flat and the neck is the widest for its size of any turtle, totally out of proportion to its body. The Matamata's mouth is a huge slit which passes under both its eyes and its tiny tube-like snout with its huge mouth. It catches and eats large numbers of fishes by waiting for them to swim by, and then opening its mouth suddenly to incredible size. The fish are sucked in with the inrush of water. Its powerful jaws snap shut with a jerk similar to that of the Alligator Snapping Turtle and the Matamata has its meal and is soon foraging for more prey. Even newly hatched Matamatas only a few inches in length show this same feeding ability. The Matamatas are strictly

33. *A plant-choked swamp with a seasonal overflow of water is a likely place to find turtles searching for food.*

side-necked or Pleurodira turtles and their heads are always at an angle to their bodies. (ILLUSTRATION 31.)

In spite of the largely carnivorous species, the overwhelming mass of food eaten by the vast majority of turtles throughout the world is plant material.

All of the larger turtles, both land tortoises and sea turtles eat vast quantities of plants. The Galapagos turtles can be seen in films and videos, as well as in zoos, munching away on green leaves, thick cactus leaves, and fruit.

While all turtles have a similar digestive system (ILLUSTRATION 29), there are wide differences between varieties, depending on their habitats and food supplies. Generally, species dependent on animal material (such as fish, frogs and crustaceans) have shorter intestines and strong stomachs. Those species which eat tough, fibrous plant leaves and stems have longer intestines and stone-grinding stomachs.

The turtles swallow small stones that remain in their stomachs and aid in grinding down the tough plant parts so they can be digested.

The intestine of a typical pond turtle shows its wide sources of food. All turtles have all of the fingerlike projections through their intestines through which the liquid and digested food are absorbed by the reptile's bloodstream. (ILLUSTRATION 32.)

Turtles living on or near the barren rocks of North American coasts eat lichens and mosses, which they usually find in the woodland in very early spring and late fall. Probably the most widely favored of all foods, although not the most easily caught, are insects.

Although it is not well-known, one of the most common foods of young freshwater and sea turtles are the tiny crustaceans, such as the nearly microscopic Daphnia or freshwater flea and the Fairy Shrimp, which teem in sun-soaked freshwater and brackish water ponds by the millions in midsummer and early fall. They are often vital to the survival of a brood of hatching turtles in their first few months of life.

The supply of food determines the number and health of turtles in a particular environment. Many times, changes in water quality, the loss of farmland to development, and consequent destruction of plants and insects will have the most immediate effect upon the number and kinds of turtles in an environment. The turtles are the first creatures to be missed in an area, and it is due to food supply being depleted. Loss of food (insects and plants) is not obvious immediately, but that does force a decline in turtle population.

34. *The great Galapagos Tortoise, now one of the world's most endangered and protected species, is here feasting on leaves and fruit. Some of the rarer groups are now down to only a few dozen individuals. They are strictly vegetarians and may live for more than 100 years.*

7. How Do Turtles Find Their Food?

Turtles locate their food with keen and highly specialized senses. Turtles have very keen eyesight, they see colors and can distinguish even the slightest movement. (ILLUSTRATION 35.) Some, like the Matamata, have reflecting features in the backs of their eyes so that, like other animals active at night, they see objects at much lower light levels than our human eyes can. Other turtle species can see light in the infrared range, which is invisible to human eyes, but which helps them to detect food our eyes could

35. Their eyes are very keen and turtles continually extend their heads and rotate their field of vision. The eyes and nostrils of turtles are placed as far forward on the skull as those of any vertebrate.

not distinguish. Not all turtles have the same size eyes located in the same places.

For example, the Common Snapping Turtle has eyes which you can see from the top if you look down on its head. But the eyes of the Alligator Snapping Turtle are placed at the sides of its

36. The Galapagos turtles are known to travel many miles between feeding grounds to find plants and watering holes inland. They can tell the direction to travel by smell.

37. This is one of the large sea turtles, the fastest moving of all turtles. They spend their entire life in salt water except for brief periods when the females come to shore to lay their eggs.

head, lower down, so you cannot see its eyes when you look down on its head from above.

The placement of all of the turtle's major sense organs are in the front of its head, so that even when the head is withdrawn into its shell, the turtle can still detect objects and activities directly in front of it. The placement of the eyes and nostrils at the front of the skull is easy to see. They are further ahead on the skull than in any other group of reptiles or amphibians.

Sea turtles have an additional transparent covering over their eyes, which enables them to see through the water at the surf out onto the beach to distinguish objects. Freshwater turtles are also able to see for long distances under water, like their seagoing relatives.

Sea turtles have one other unique feature. They take in a vast amount of salt from the ocean water they swallow and from the food they eat. Special glands in their eye sockets, similar to tear glands, clear some of this excess salt out of their system. These glands were discovered by a Swiss anatomist named Harder in 1694, and they are named for him: Harderian glands.

Turtles' sense of smell is very well developed, possibly their most extensive sense next to their vision. Many instances have been recorded where turtles could be attracted from considerable distances by strong-smelling foods, such as cheese, rotten fish, or stale eggs. (ILLUSTRATION 36.) Certain small freshwater turtles of North America and Asia give off a putrid, musky smell

38. *A slight movement in the background was enough to send a vibration to these two Painted Turtles. They withdrew into their shells as if on command.*

themselves when disturbed. This was thought at one time to be a way of attracting mates, but it seems more likely that it is a defense against predators, such as raccoons and possums which dislike the musky odor and taste.

Turtles have no external ears, such as mice and cats have, or even any similar to frogs'. But they do have extensive organs for vibration detection inside their skulls. They certainly do not hear sounds in the same way that human beings, dogs, or cats do. They are more sensitive to vibrations in the ground or water over longer distances than humans are. It may be that the great land tortoises of the Galapagos can actually hear or feel the vibrations of the earth when their group walks.

Turtles use their sense of vibration to obtain some of their food. Box turtles will stand in one spot at the edge of a meadow and tap the ground with one forefoot and then the other. They do this for a dozen or so taps at a time. The vibration disturbs the earthworms beneath the soil and they come to the surface to escape it; there

39. *Pond turtles in a well constructed enclosure with plants and perches move from location to location in and out of the water to control their temperatures.*

they are eaten by the box turtle. A large adult turtle can catch ten or more earthworms at a session this way.

All turtles are voiceless, except for some males of a few species which make unusual sounds, largely hissing noises, while mating. In the King James Bible of 1611 in the poem *The Song of Solomon (2:12)*, "And the voice of the turtle is heard in the land" appears. This has led to many misunderstandings for centuries. When we look at the statements which precede this strange phrase:

> *"The flowers appear on the earth,*
> *the time of the singing of birds is come,*
> *and the voice of the turtle is heard in the land."*

It becomes clear that the "turtle" mentioned is not the reptile at all but a bird, the well-known "turtle dove."

The nerves from all three sense organs of turtles, sight, smell, and vibration, appear to pass into related areas of their brains.

Just how these three senses are understood by turtles is very much of a mystery. But it is clear that it is difficult to sneak up on a turtle sunning itself on a rock or by the edge of a pond. It seems that if turtles do not see or smell us approaching, then the vibrations we make as we walk or crawl reaches them well before we do. Usually they silently slide into the water at our approach. (ILLUSTRATION 38.)

While turtles are usually seen moving slowly and carefully on land, almost all are good swimmers. And in fact, many can divert the air in their lungs to one side or the other and alter their angle and depth in the water by doing so. This action of the air-filled lungs inside the shell is similar to the swim-bladder of fishes by which they can control their level in the water.

40. Galapagos
Tortoises
mating.

8. A Turtle Is Born

All turtles hatch from eggs. Different species lay different numbers of eggs from two, by some small pond varieties, to several
hundred, by the largest sea species. The eggs vary in size from
slightly larger than marbles to the size of tennis balls. Unlike the
eggs of birds, which they resemble, they are more leathery and
not as hard and round. They are all white to slightly gray in color.
Some are actually oblong, like the eggs of snakes. They are also
different from birds' eggs in that they cannot be rotated or rolled
while developing. Male turtles in mating approach the females
from behind and push an organ out of their cloaca into the
receptor organ in the female's cloaca. While all freshwater and
land turtles mate on land (ILLUSTRATION 40) sea turtles can mate in
water. Most turtles mate once a year after reaching maturity.
Conflicts between males during the breeding season are common
among most species. Some of these are quite fierce and leave the
older males battle-scarred, with chips and chunks actually bitten
out of their shells, and possibly toes and tails missing. On the

41. A southern Box Turtle has dug a nest to lay its eggs in, and now the hatchling is emerging. The process took almost 5 hours.

other hand, a few species are known to perform graceful mating rituals, similar to some lizards and even as dramatic as birds.

When most terrestrial turtles are ready to mate, the males will follow closely behind the females and frequently approach close enough to butt their shells together. This may be accompanied by extending the head fairly far out of the shell and waving it from side to side, or up and down. Females of many species will stand completely still and retract their heads and feet into their shells while mating.

While normally voiceless, this is the one time that male turtles will give off a groaning sound. Male freshwater aquatic turtles of North America will mate in shallow water, as in ponds, where the male and female will swim after each other for hours and even days until they actually join their cloacas and mating takes place.

The female will only climb out on land when she actually is going to excavate her nest and deposit the eggs, which may be from a day to a month after mating, depending on environmental conditions.

Commonly, many turtles release special scents called pheromones which cause appropriate responses from adults of the opposite sex. Many types of musk turtles do this. However, it is not clear that the musky odor associated with these turtles is, in fact, the pheromone. These chemicals act as stimulants and work very effectively to bring adults together when it is time to mate.

42. A turtle egg.

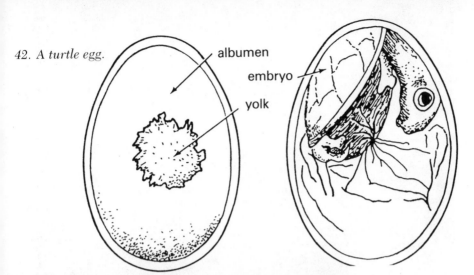

albumen

embryo

yolk

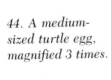

43. Live turtle eggs inside an incubator.

44. A medium-sized turtle egg, magnified 3 times.

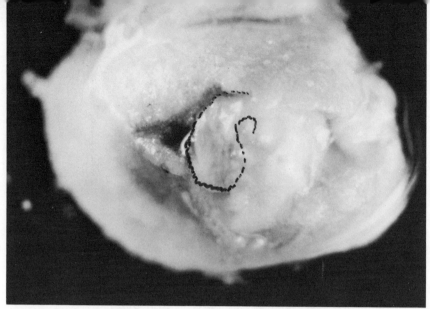

45. *Embryo in 10–15 mm stage (shell removed). The head is shown in outline.*

Female turtles are able to carry live male sperm cells in special sacs near their cloaca for *years* after one mating! There are records of turtles laying fertile eggs for up to four years after a single mating. Females will always look for suitable nesting sites, before laying their eggs in the ground, but then they give no care or attention to the eggs. Even the great sea turtles must come up onto beaches to dig nests and lay their eggs. Turtle eggs hatch in from a month to three months, depending on species and temperature. Some types of eggs can even stay in the ground through the winter and hatch the next spring when the weather turns warmer. But most hatch the same season.

Turtle hatching is complicated. At base, each turtle egg is a self-contained life-support system in miniature. It has an outer

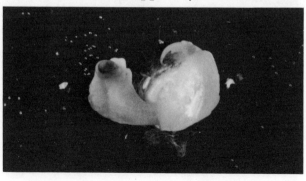

46. *In this 15–20-mm embryo, note the large head, small cap-like shell, and long tail.*

47. A 20-mm embryo seen from the under side. Note plastron and fully formed limbs.

shell which can pass gasses in and out, but retains water and other fluids. In the egg is a developing embryo and a prepackaged food supply, the yolk.

The backbone, nerves, and circulatory system of the embryo form before the external parts. It is still difficult to make out the head, body, and limb buds but they are growing rapidly. Soon the earliest signs of the upper shell, the carapace, appear (ILLUSTRATION 45). When the embryo has reached a length of 15 mm (millimetres) the head starts to grow and soon is nearly as big as the body. The shoulder and hip bones are growing out of the spine, with the ribs along the sides. However, soon the carapace will overtake and fuse to the ribs, shoulders, and hips almost as though the embryo were wrapping itself into a box (ILLUSTRATION 47).

Soon the lower shell, the *plastron*, will catch up with the

48. Back and head of a 20-mm embryo. Note fully formed scutes.

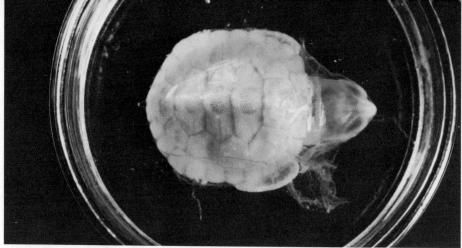

49. *Top view of 25- to 30-mm embryo shows faint coloration patterns on the scutes and the embryonic membrane covering the embryo.*

50. *In this underside view of a 25- to 30-mm embryo, plastron has the central space where vitelline veins pass through the shell to carry yolk to the embryo. The small knob on the pointed snout is the shell caruncle, which will be used to break a hole in the shell.*

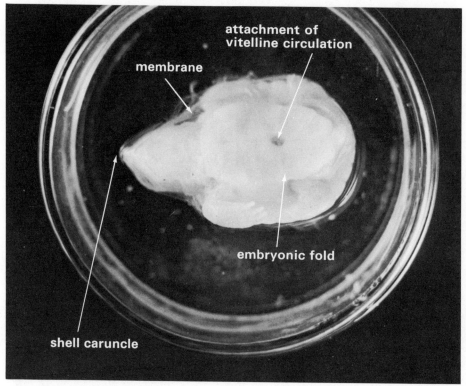

growth of the embryo and bridges between carapace and plastron will form. The eyes and the brain areas that control sight now grow very rapidly and soon appear to be out of proportion to the rest of the little body. The forefeet and hindfeet are now fully formed and the claws are beginning to appear (ILLUSTRATION 47).

Most turtles have shields or *scutes* of a tough, flexible material similar to horn. The margins of the plates never fall along the same lines as those of the scutes, so the shell is very rigid and strong. This construction is called *lamination* and has many of the properties of man-made plywood. The higher the curve or pitch of a turtle's shell, the stronger it is. The scutes and pitch can be seen well in the later stages of the embryo (ILLUSTRATION 48).

Now the embryo begins to move and the nerves start to take on their functions. The limbs begin to take on coloration and the plastron hardens. The upper shell or carapace has now grown over the limbs completely and the small turtle is a fully formed replica of the adult. The remains of the embryonic membranes still enshroud the whole turtle (ILLUSTRATION 49) and a sharp horny knob develops on the end of the beak-like upper jaw (ILLUSTRATION 50).

The vitelline circulation still carries the all-important foodstuff from the yolk sac to the young turtle.

When fully developed, the young turtle begins to break through the tough outer shell with a special hook-like attachment on its upper beak, called an egg *caruncle*. It may take nearly a full day to break through the shell. (ILLUSTRATION 41.)

At this point the body is mostly cartilage and not yet turned to bone. When it takes its first few breaths it expands its lungs and breaks its shell even further. During this time of intense effort, the vibrations it sends through the ground are sensed by the other hatching turtles in the nest and all begin to work together to dig through the soil above them to the surface. This is especially important for sea turtle hatchlings as they must get into the surf as soon as possible. It is during this migration of tiny turtles to the sea that millions are eaten by birds and beach predators, such as rats and crabs.

One of the great mysteries of turtle life was how hatchling sea turtles find their way back to the same beaches where they were hatched years before to lay their eggs when they mature. The

This active hatchling turtle is in the 40-mm stage. Note that it already has a bright pattern of coloration.

answer seems to be that during the first day of their life on the beach, they taste the sand! Since the sand in each region is slightly different because of mineral content, algae, and other factors, their memory of the sand where they were born becomes implanted, and they are able to navigate back to it years later. But there are many, many aspects of how turtles navigate in the open sea and survive in other difficult environments which are still to be discovered.

Turtles, like other reptiles, have no fixed speed at which they grow or mature. Typically they take from 3 to 10 years to reach breeding age, and they may be various sizes by that age. In good environmental conditions, they grow slowly at best and take up to a year to double in size from their birth weight and length. (ILLUSTRATION 51.) Contrary to what you may read elsewhere, turtles can be hatched in captivity, but the eggs must be laid on dry land and quickly covered over with a mixture of wet sand and some light mulch. The eggs must then be kept warm and moist,

The markings through the head and eye of this young red-eared turtle help to break up its silhouette. Its broken pattern, called protective coloration, helps it blend into the pond vegetation where it thrives.

but not immersed in water or they will drown. It is a tricky process and best left to experts. But many turtles are hatched today in protected areas so that their natural populations can be increased to avoid extinction.

A *half-grown Western painted turtle, a very rapid swimmer and strong walker, spends most of its life in ponds and lakes.*

51. *Three generations of Box Turtles. The smallest turtle (at left) is only a month old, the one in the middle a year, and the adult (on the right) five years.*

9. How Big Do Turtles Get and How Long Do They Live?

One of the smallest species is the Muhlenberg Box Turtle of the Middle Atlantic states which rarely exceeds 3½ inches (9cm) in length. But many other freshwater pond turtles of the United States are common at this size (ILLUSTRATION 51.)

After being hunted to extinction on many tropical islands, only two groups of large land tortoises are left in the world. The most famous are (first) the various species of the Galapagos Islands off the western coast of Ecuador, and (second) the Seychelles Islands species in the Indian Ocean off the north coast of Madagascar. The Galapagos Tortoise has a shell nearly 4 feet in length (1.1m)

52. *The common Yellow Bellied Pond Turtle, the most widely sold and kept as pets, are found in one color variation or another over much of the United States. They are typically between 3 and 4 inches (10cm) in length.*

and weighs several hundred pounds. (ILLUSTRATION 34, PAGE 33). But the average size for all freshwater and land turtles is about 12 inches (30cm) and a weight well under 10 pounds (ILLUSTRATION 53.) The largest of all living species are the sea turtles, called Leatherbacks, which grow to 6 feet in length and weigh over a ton.

Turtles can keep growing throughout their lives. In the days of wooden sailing ships, sea turtles of enormous size were reported being caught by sailors. While turtles half again larger than the average of their species are known, these giants have become rarer and rarer throughout the twentieth century. But whatever their ultimate size, turtles are the longest living of all vertebrates—scientific accounts verify a giant tortoise reaching 152 years of age. Even Alligator Snapping Turtles in zoos have lived for 75 and even 80 years in captivity. Small land tortoises, like the common Box Turtle, are documented to have lived 35

53. This Gopher Tortoise is about average size for all common freshwater and land turtles. It is about 12 inches (30cm) long and weighs less than 10 pounds. While most turtles this size can live to 40 or 50 years of age, very few do in nature.

years. But most turtles in natural environments probably live only about half that long.

The age of individual turtles can best be estimated by looking carefully at their shells. Most will show signs of wear, numerous mating battles, and close-calls from dogs and cats, such signs as scratches and breaks on their lower shells, the plastron. (ILLUS-TRATION 54.) Old males will often have lost toes and chips out of their beaks or the back portions of the carapace. Females usually have pieces missing from their back carapaces caused by overly aggressive males, and many have whole vertebrae missing from their tails. Land tortoises often have feet worn down to stumps, or bitten by predators.

While turtles do add annual rings to their scutes each year of their life cycle, these are not easily determined and, unlike tree rings, cannot be counted on to give an accurate age.

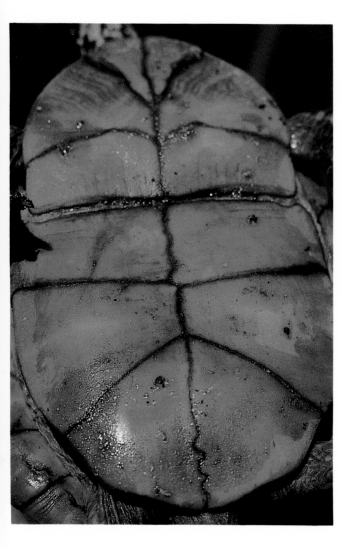

54. The wear and tear on their shells is the best indication of the age of a turtle. This Box Turtle has minimal wear on its plastron, showing it to be no more than 4 years old.

10. How Do Turtles Adapt to Weather Changes?

Many turtles live in environments where the seasons change. Even in most tropical areas there are rainy seasons and dry seasons, but in all of North America, Europe, and much of Asia, there are four distinct seasons. Spring starts with melting of the ice, resulting in the streams and rivers running with torrents of fresh water. As the first forest and field plants appear through the

55. *Desert tortoises often seek shade during the middle of the day and the "gopher" species can even tunnel into the sand to seek cooler temperatures.*

melting snow, turtles end their long winter hibernation and begin to seek mates. It is at this point when we first begin to find them wandering through the woods and fields, and even over lawns and gardens. Most turtles have small territories, only a few hundred square yards in which they forage and feed. But during the breeding season, the males will wander far from their usual habitats. As food becomes more abundant, they feed voraciously and the females begin to nest and lay their eggs.

As spring progresses and summer begins, the turtles sun themselves on every available log or rock, but must keep watch for predators. Also, they must balance their need for warmth and sun with their need to keep from overheating. While food is now plentiful and their eggs are developing in their nests, the adults often gather in groups to sun or shade themselves. This is the season of the year when favorite foods become so abundant that turtles can actually pick and choose.

56. *The leaves have fallen after the killing frost in the eastern United States. A Soft-Shelled Turtle with its typical leathery hide at the edge of its carapace and long tube-like nose, looks in the fall grass for frogs and toads to eat. It will soon look for a den to hibernate. The last animals still active before winter will feast on bugs and berries.*

57. *The Galapagos Tortoise's high-domed shell and heavy scutes insulate it from the hot desert sun and retain its fresh water inside.*

For many years there were groups of wild blackberry bushes in the woods beside the author's house. Whenever children went to pick some, they almost always found Box Turtles under the branches with the telltale purple juice staining their beaks. They had been eating the berries which had fallen. These same fruit-loving turtles would get into rows of strawberries and gobble them down. By summer's end the turtles, both land dwellers and water dwellers, have put on size and weight, and the new generation has hatched from the eggs.

As fall comes on and the daily period of sunlight grows shorter, the nights get cooler and the plants go to seed. The insects are fat with eggs and the turtles gorge themselves to build up their last reserves of energy for the winter. When the vegetation begins to die back, the turtles move to their places of hibernation for the winter. (ILLUSTRATION 56.) The turtles will stay active long beyond almost any other hibernating animals. The few turtles which are still out and about are storing their energy in the form of fat, and leave their digestive tracts empty to winter over.

58. *The "saddleback" type of Galapagos Tortoise is one of the rarest of the great tortoises. The rolled-back carapace allows the tortoise to reach its head higher among the bushes and trees for its food.*

During winter the fresh water freezes throughout most of North America for some period of time. In the more northerly areas it may stay frozen for three or more months at a stretch. During this time, some of the turtles' most unusual adaptations become evident. Even though they are commonly called "cold-blooded," this in no way means that turtle blood freezes along with the fresh water. While the turtles do become sluggish, they have been seen walking under thick ice in ponds and in stream beds. The freshwater is trapped under the ice. But the pond turtles are all hibernating in the mud below the bottom of the pond and around the margins.

Larger species living in northern climates can stay active until the temperature falls to 23 degrees F (-10 degrees C). Since water cannot be compacted any tighter than it can at -4 degrees C, water will remain a liquid below the thickest ice. So virtually all freshwater turtles of northern climates can survive in winter in deep water. And since turtles can slow down their use of oxygen, they can stay under water for days or weeks at a time. They can also slow down the rate of their heartbeat. In fact, rates of one beat per nine minutes have been recorded!

But only recently an even stranger adaptation has been discovered: it seems that young pond turtles buried in the mud in their shallow ponds, can freeze solid until all their life processes are slowed to a stop, and still survive when they thaw in the spring. This is made possible by special antifreezing proteins in their blood. So even small turtles have wonderful ways to survive the harshest winter.

Finally the ice thaws, the snow melts, and another spring begins.

59. A rich wildlife thrives in these woods and along this stream. The trees drop their leaves in the autumn to add to the abundance of nuts and seeds. The turtles have plenty to feed on.

60. The adult Burmese Tortoise has concave bony scutes on its carapace, but not on its plastron, a peculiar and unexplained adaptation.

11. Special Adaptations

There are many other special ways in which turtles have overcome challenges in their habitats, besides climates, food and seasonal conditions. Unique conditions make their lives very different even in the same climate somewhere else.

The great tortoises still found in the Galapagos and the Seychelles Islands are typical. The standard Galapagos tortoise (ILLUSTRATION 57) lives chiefly on cactus and other fleshy dry-weather, warm-sunshine plants on its nearly desert islands. However, the tortoise can, and must, travel a considerable distance from its food supply to get water. It has become able over centuries to retain water for long periods of time and to maintain a regular temperature inside its high, domed shell. However, it still primarily eats plants and leaves at, or just above, ground level.

It has relatives on some of the other islands—at least 14 different types are known—that have to reach higher and eat different types of plants. One very definite adaptation for doing this is the turned-up "saddle-back" front of the carapace, which allows the tortoise to raise its head high. (ILLUSTRATION 58.)

61. *The common tortoise of the American Desert not only has a unique coloration but many internal adaptations to its hot, dry environment, which is hostile to most forms of life.*

One unexplained oddity is the tendency of older specimens of the Burmese Tortoise, a species of Geochelone, to have the individual bony scutes on its carapace turn outward at the edge like tiny oriental roof tiles. The scutes on the plastron are not concave like this, but are convex on the surface. (ILLUSTRATION 60.)

Desert-dwelling tortoises must be careful to conserve water. Many varieties living in areas of the great American and Mexican desert, where it may rain only a few times in an entire year, have special adaptations for this severe climate. Most interesting is their ability to derive water from the cactus leaves which they eat. The American Desert Tortoise (ILLUSTRATION 61) retains almost pure water in its extended bladder from the scrubby desert plants it eats. But freshwater species have another problem. Unlike their saltwater relatives, they do not have to keep saltwater out and rid their bodies of the excess salt within; they have to keep the salts within their bodies from leaking out into the fresh water where they live. This is done through efficient kidneys and other organs controlling the output of salts from the blood. (ILLUSTRATION 62.) Both freshwater and saltwater turtles must maintain the proper balance of salts inside their bodies with those in the water outside their bodies.

Some species pass between both environments. The best known is the Diamond-Backed Terrapin of the eastern coast of the United States. (ILLUSTRATION 63.) This species has been famous for its flavor in soups and stews since early colonial times. It thrives in brackish water where the many small bays and rivers of the eastern United States meet the Atlantic Ocean. These turtles are so common along seashore roads, and even major highways during the spring breeding season, that many thousands are killed by vehicles. They range from tidal pools at low tide to pine forests and small streams running with dark brown cedar water. All of these habitats are different in their chemistry and plant growth, yet the Diamond-Back thrives in each of them, and on whatever food is available.

Turtles with a special set of adaptations are found in fresh water around the world. These are in Soft-shelled turtles, so called

62. *Water turtles are frequently counter shaded, which means that they appear dark from above, but are mottled with light and dark color contrasts when seen from below. These colorings help conceal them in the waters where they live.*

63. The well-known Diamond-Backed Terrapin not only varies in shade from one local area to another, but it has many dots and dashes of color to break up its outline and make it harder to distinguish from its background for both prey and predator.

because they have a flat and somewhat reduced, almost round, carapace, covered by a thick leathery hide. They also have a long tube-like nose and a small pointed head. (ILLUSTRATION 64.)

64. A pair of Soft-Shelled Turtles. These are typical of southern rivers and are very aggressive and strictly carnivorous.

65. *A Musk or Mud Turtle blends in with a tree stump in a wood lot.*

These turtles are able to take breaths of air through their tube nostrils while keeping the rest of their head submerged. Highly aggressive, they will actually bite a person, a dog, or cat, quicker and with greater agility than the notorious Alligator Snapping Turtles which may be ten times their size. The Soft-Shells are excellent swimmers and prefer to spend most of their lives in the water, only coming out to breed, lay their eggs, and sun themselves. In their environments in North America, Africa, and Asia, they are strictly carnivorous and can chase and catch fish.

Similar to the Soft-shelled turtles, the very rare Plateless Turtle of the Fly River of southern New Guinea is perhaps the finest swimmer of all freshwater species. It has large seal-like flippers and only two toes, similar to sea turtles. It lives in the vast expanses of river water in its environment. Plateless Turtles swim with broad strokes of their wide fins and make it look incredibly easy. They seem to always be in motion and can pursue and eat fish at an amazing rate. They appear to actually swim faster than the larger sea turtles. They only grow to about 18 inches (45cm) and have a very reduced carapace and plastron, almost like sea turtles.

66. *A Box Turtle sunning on a block in a turtle tank. It takes on a rock-like appearance with no movement, even when approached.*

68. *One of the small hinge-back tortoises of Africa, seriously endangered by the expansion of farmland.*

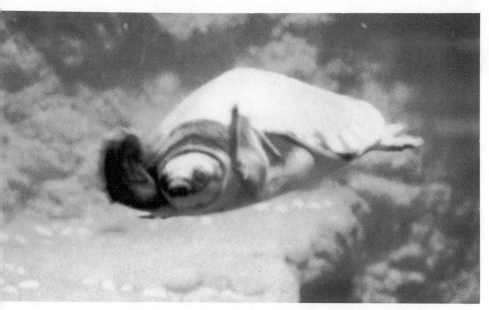

67. *The rare and endangered Plateless Turtle of the Fly River of New Guinea swims very fast and has swift movements under water with its huge, almost fish-like fins. Here it is stroking towards the camera with its overly large front fins about to take a sweeping breaststroke.*

12. Can the Turtle Survive?

For millions and millions of years turtles survived within their hard boxes of bone and with their many kinds of special adaptations. However, the growth of human populations and the draining of ponds and swamps have limited their food supplies and taken away their habitats at an alarming rate. In addition, the hunting of turtle eggs and adult animals for food in many tropical countries where turtles breed has brought some species to the edges of extinction.

Perhaps not all species of turtles now living will survive even to the year 2000, but many of the common ones will if we provide them with as much space and open areas as we can. A turtle's first line of defense is just being left alone. Most of those in temperate climates will just be passed by and taken for a rock or stone if they do not move (ILLUSTRATION 66.) Most of the woodland and pond

69, 70. *Two different desert tortoises now becoming threatened by human intrusion into their habitat.*

varieties just blend in with the coloration of their surroundings. (ILLUSTRATION 65.) While it is good to point out turtles when we see them in their natural environment, there is no reason why they must be picked up or moved. Over a period of days or weeks, the same individual turtles come back and in the same place again and again.

In all countries, turtles are under pressure and turtle populations are falling. Many of the desert turtles are particularly
susceptible to extinction. They are killed by machines seeking to
develop the land, and by animals, such as rats and mice which
accompany human dwellings and activities. Small forest turtles
found in Africa are particularly hard pressed by the cutting down
of trees and the conversion of the woodland habitat to farmland
(ILLUSTRATION 68.)

The most severely affected tortoises are those of the Galapagos
and Seychelles islands which are related to many species once
found all across the Pacific and Indian Ocean islands. Small
colonies were hunted to extinction for food by sailors in the days
of sailing ships, when fresh foods had to be obtained from any
source. Modern scientists have discovered the remains of extinct
turtle species on a number of tropical islands and many different
varieties are in the collections of museums. However, the great
beasts themselves are slowly losing their habitats to human
settlements and to the animals which humans brought with
them, not simply dogs, cats, rats and mice, but the small and
voracious mongoose. All of these hunt and eat turtle eggs. Zoos
around the world are trying to maintain populations of the great
tortoises as they disappear in the wild.

At present, the American tortoises of the southwestern desert
are being deprived of their sand habitats by building and development, as we have seen in other parts of the world. But one
additional problem is the frequent use of small motorcycles and
other gasoline-powered vehicles by millions of vacationers. The
noise and dust of these vehicles and their destruction of the
sparse desert plants make the need for large conservation areas
absolutely necessary. (ILLUSTRATIONS 69, 70.)

The most common turtle in North America is the Painted
Turtle, found in great numbers in all of the ponds and rivers of the
southern states. Aside from the draining of its habitats, the chief
threat to this species is the enormous number—literally
millions—that are captured and sold in the pet trade each year.
This brings us to the subject of keeping turtles in captivity.

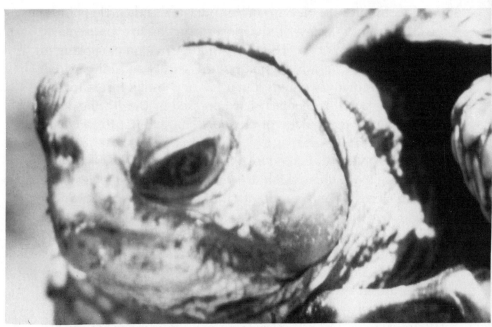

71. *A pet turtle suffering from poor nutrition; one of many vitamin deficiencies has caused the cyst in the gland behind the eye.*

13. How Should We Keep and Watch Turtles?

Many types of turtles can be kept in captivity. But there are three basic rules for doing so. The first is to provide plenty of space, light, and adequate heat. The second is to keep the turtles clean. The third is to provide them with a varied diet. You do not need a fancy container for a small turtle. Any container which is waterproof and at least one foot by one foot, 1 ft square (30 cm) will work. Remember that turtles are not necessarily community animals unless in their breeding season, so one will do perfectly well by itself.

But there must be provision for the turtle to move from water a few inches deep to dry land within the container. It must also be able to move from a sunlit area to shade during the day. In climates where there is very little sunlight through the fall and winter, an electric light should be provided. Turtles must have light to provide themselves with vitamin A. The best outdoor turtle tanks are 30 to 100 gallons with plant pots and places to swim.

Turtle diets must be varied. Commercial turtle foods are woefully inadequate. A small amount of food—the amount a turtle can completely consume in 30 minutes should be its diet each day, and served preferably at about the same time. Raw ground or chopped meat, fish, or fowl, along with fruit and vegetables are sufficient. More aggressive species and larger water turtles will often take small quantities of commercial dog or cat food. If the turtle is fed in its living container, then that area must be cleaned out every few days to prevent rotten food and decaying feces from fouling the water.

One very important aspect of turtle nutrition is the addition of vitamin supplements. (ILLUSTRATION 71.) Usually the same commercial products made for puppies or kittens will work very well; some calcium or bonemeal may be added to the food every few days.

The best way to view turtles is in their natural environment. Occasionally some may be brought into the classroom for a week or two, but they should be returned to their environment after they have been observed. Lots of interesting things are to be seen as turtles go about their life cycles. The best way to observe them is to locate some in your area and watch them frequently throughout the year.

AFTERWORD

Why are the wetlands so important to the environment?

Wetlands are the swamps and marshes that form a boundary between solid land and waterways. As water passes through a wetland it gives off some of its sediment, phosphates and pollutants, which would otherwise travel on to clog the rivers, inlets, lakes, brooks and ponds. They are the breeding grounds for aquatic life—for turtles and frogs as well as fishes and waterfowl. The wetlands absorb floodwaters and reduce shoreline erosion.

Government supervision of the environment, especially the wetlands, is becoming more and more of a political issue and it is imperative that everyone from the youngest student to the oldest voters learn about the inhabitants of the wetlands whose life will become endangered by the crowding of the environment by creeping civilization.

—THE EDITORS

ACKNOWLEDGMENTS

The author and publisher wish to thank all those who wrote comments and suggestions regarding "A Turtle Is Born," the predecessor to this book. All photographs are by the author with additional images courtesy of: Palmer Paist, Ardella Reed, Sam Saylor, Tony La Gruth, Marjorie T. Forrest, and Doris Friedman. The manuscript was prepared by Sara Jane White.

Index